KIOSK

KIOSK

Hans Magnus Enzensberger

TRANSLATED BY
MICHAEL HAMBURGER

with additional translations by
HANS MAGNUS ENZENSBERGER

BLOODAXE BOOKS

ISBN: 1 85224 385 6

First published 1997 by
Bloodaxe Books Ltd,
P.O. Box 1SN,
Newcastle upon Tyne NE99 1SN.

Bloodaxe Books Ltd acknowledges
the financial assistance of Northern Arts.

Thanks are due to the Arts Council of England
for providing a translation grant for this book.

Cover printing by J. Thomson Colour Printers Ltd, Glasgow.

Printed in Great Britain by
Cromwell Press Ltd, Broughton Gifford, Melksham, Wiltshire.

Acknowledgements

The original German edition of this book was first published by Surhkamp Verlag, Frankfurt am Main, in 1995. Additional translations by Hans Magnus Enzensberger are marked [HME]; all other translations are by Michael Hamburger.

Acknowledgements are due to the editors of the following publications in which some of these translations first appeared: *Agenda, Nineties Poetry, PN Review, Poetry Review* and *Stand*.

Contents

HISTORICAL PATCHWORK

Kiosk

At the nearest corner
the three elderly sisters
in their wooden booth.
Blithely they offer
murder poison war
to a nice clientèle
for breakfast.

Fine weather today. Homeless folk
eating dog biscuits. Property owners
choking in villas
beneath Tanagra figurines,
and other living creatures
who at sunrise punctually
disappear in banks,

weird as the mammoth
with its ringed tusks
and the praying mantis.
They don't disturb me.
I too like to do
my shopping at the Fates.

The War, like

It glitters like the broken beer bottle in the sun
at the bus stop in front of the old people's home

It rustles like the ghost writer's manuscript
at the peace conference

It flickers like the bluish reflection of the TV screen
on sleep-walking faces

It smells like the steel of the apparatus in fitness clubs
like the bodyguard's breath at the airport

It blows like the chairman's speech
It inflates like the fatwah in the Ayatollah's mouth

It chirps like the video game on the schoolboy's disk
It sparkles like the chips at the bank's computer centre

It expands like the puddle behind the slaughterhouse

Breathes
rustles
inflates
smells

like

Privileged Instructions

It is forbidden to set fire to persons.

It is forbidden to set fire to persons in possession of a valid
residence permit.

It is forbidden to set fire to persons who comply with Government
regulations and are in possession of a valid residence permit.

It is forbidden to set fire to persons not suspected of endangering
the constitution and security of the German Federal Republic.

It is forbidden to set fire to persons whose behaviour and attitudes are
not conducive to that suspicion.

More specifically, juveniles, too, who in view of deficient leisure
facilities and in ignorance of the relevant regulations or
because of difficulties of orientation are psychically endangered,
are not permitted to set fire to persons indiscriminately.

Indeed that course is urgently inadvisable in consideration of the
German Federal Republic's reputation abroad.

It is not seemly.

It is not usual.

It is not to become the rule.

It is not necessary.

No one is obliged to do it.

No one is to be blamed if he or she refrains from setting fire to persons.

It is everyone's basic right to refuse to do so.

Relevant applications should be submitted to the regulatory office
responsible.

NB. Anyone translating this text into another language is requested to try substituting
the official designation of his or her country for the German Federal Republic. This
footnote is to be retained in a translation.

Translator's note: This would call for a translation much more free than the one
provided. It is the reader who is invited to try out that substitution in his or her
mind, with appropriate modifications of terminology and reference.

The Rich

Wherever do they keep on coming from,
these luxurious hordes! After every collapse
they've crept out of the ruins,
unmoved; through every eye of a needle
they've slipped,
rich in number, good heels and blessings.

Those wretches. Nobody likes them.
Their burden bows them down.
They offend us,
are to blame for everything,
can't help it,
must be got rid of.

We've tried everything.
We've preached to them,
we've implored them,
and only when there was no other way
blackmailed, expropriated, plundered them.
We have left them to bleed
and put them against the wall.

But no sooner did we lower the rifle
and seated ourselves in their armchairs
than we knew, incredulous
at first, but then with a sigh of relief:
we too were irrepressible.
Yes, yes, one gets used to anything.
Till it happens again.

Economic Life

Someone is paid
for determining policy,
for slaughtering,
for interpreting Kierkegaard,
for lying down in bed,
for depressing piano keys,
for donating his semen,
for making progress at last
on the Lipotropin synthesis,
for truncheoning, cooking,
ironing, scoring goals,
for disappearing at last.

The Tin Plate

About poverty all has been said:
that it's tenacious, sticky, persistent
and of no interest to anybody
save the poor. It is boring.
It has too much to worry about
to complain about boredom.
Like dirt, it is to be found
way down. It's contagious,
smelly, a nuisance.

Its omnipresence is striking.
It seems to partake of eternity.
Attributes which are divine.
Helpers and saints seek it.
Monks and nuns are betrothed to it.
With the rest of us,
all our lives on the run,
poverty catches up
at the next street-corner,

unmoving, unmoved, majestic,
tin-plate in hand.

[HME]

An Observation on Shifts in Functional Elites

This abrasive noise,
a scraping by day and night,
of toes, fingers, claws –
this comes of the scratching,
the climbing, the crawling of those
who with their breath held
want to rise, high,

higher and higher, full of fear,
the fear that the sandy slope
will give way under their nails
so that down, to the place
they came from, they will slide
and the more, in their panic,
even before the brittle edge

crumbles, breaks, on all
they suppose to be below them
they start to trample,
the more, ineluctably,

downward

Old Europe

In the warm bread smell in front of the bakery
a fat magician from Guinea
under the golden pretzel offers
key-ring pendants for sale
in Graubrüdergasse.
(Who were those Greyfriars?)

Little wiry dealers
in huge trainers growling
quarrel in a language
nobody understands, by the wall
of the Holy Ghost churchyard.
(Who was the Holy Ghost?)

And then the old Bosnian woman
stretching her stiff legs
for a few minutes on a bench
in the dark-green silent courtyard
behind the dark-green portal
of the Elephant Inn, built in 1639.

Audiosignal of April 14th 1912
Noise Level $> 8\,\mu W$, signal to noise ratio $> 22\,db$

Lisping mumbling babbling whispering
snuffling fluting soughing munching
muttering jabbering cooing puffing

stammering blubbing drooling grunting
drivelling rasping piping gabbling
cackling bleating bawling howling

ringing chirping shrilling squeaking
crackling clanking grating hissing
howling whistling clattering grinding

rumbling cracking sputtering roaring
hammering thudding thundering booming
blabbing belching gurgling sloshing

stuttering whining groaning bellowing
moaning bickering gasping sighing
sobbing screeching whimpering rattling

rustling rustling rustling rustling

In Memory of Sir Hiram Maxim (1840-1916)

I (1945)

On the way to school in the ditch,
the roar of the fighter-plane swooping down,
little clouds of dust to the left, in front of us,
to the right, soundless, and only a moment later
the aircraft gun's hammering.
We did not appreciate his invention.

II (1854-1878)

Later, much later did he emerge
from an old encyclopaedia. A country boy.
Their farm in the wilderness, harassed
by bears, a long time ago. At fourteen,
a cartwright's apprentice. Sixteen hours a day
at four dollars a month. Scraped along
as a brass-founder, boxer, instrument maker,
shouting: A chronic inventor, that's me!
Improved mousetraps and curlers
and built a pneumatic merry-go-round.
His steam aeroplane, with a boiler
of 1200 pounds, three tons water-supply,
broke down under its own dead weight.
Neither did his ersatz coffee take off.
He had to wait for the Great Paris Exhibition,
a fairy-world of arc-lamps and filaments,
for the Legion of Honour and for his illumination.

III   (1881-1901)

Three years later the Prince of Wales
could inspect in the vaults of Hatton Garden
a miracle of precision:
it loaded, cocked, bolted and triggered,
opened the breech-lock, ejected the shell,
reloaded, cocked, again and again, by itself,
and the cadence was fabulous: ten rounds
per second, continuous firing.
The recoil barrel, a stroke of genius!
cried the Duke of Cambridge. Never again
will war be what it used to be!
A weapon of unprecedented elegance!
The knighthood was not long in coming.

IV   (1994)

Nowadays of course, with his masterpiece
being available in any school playground,
we fail to feel what he must have felt:
the compulsive joy of a bearded mammal
with 270 patents to his credit.
As to us, his juniors by a hundred years,
we lay low as if dead in the ditch.

[HME]

Autumn 1944

True, to the one who lay in the grass
they seemed glorious,
glittering there so high up
against the cloudless October sky,
the bomber chains, and he didn't care
about those mementos
that far away were burnt
in the mouldering loft:

antique cups and angel's hair,
Grandfather's postcards from Paris
(Oh là là) and his belt buckle
from another war,
petticoats with holes, decorations,
dolls' houses, the Psyche in plaster
and a few forgotten proofs of God
in a cigar-box —

but those corpses in the cellar
are still there.

Early Writings

Today she came back to me
after forty years,
in the full light of afternoon.
What became of it,
the tattered volume
she gave me at that time?
The pathos of those sentences,
her fluttering hand
had underlined in red ink?

The Early Writings –
no one had heard of them
at that time, in Germany.
Grey was the dust
of the fifties.
Freckles
in mid-winter,
a touching impatience.

Years ago someone told me,
whoever it was, years ago,
on the telephone, by the way,
that she'd killed herself.
Nothing reminds me of her
today, on this warm Wednesday
in May, not even
a book that reading tattered.

Ode to Stupidity

Heavenly power that hides in the folds of the tribal brain,
bottomless dowry to the human race *in saecula saeculorum*,

numberless as the Milky Way you are
and multiple as grass.

Mighty twin sister of intelligence, holding hands
together with her you celebrate the dim-witted palaver.

Yes, it's impressive, how you inspire us in transformations
ever new, as feminine daftness and masculine idiocy,

how you shine from the bloodshot eyes of the hooligan
and trip along in upper-class arrogance clearing its throat,

and how you waft at us with a bedraggled Muse's bad breath
and as polysyllabic delirium in the philosophy seminar.

What would the efficient man be without you, stick-, straw-,
          goose-brained Stupidity
that, fiery, runs through his veins like an overdose of amphetamine,

and the researcher without his idée fixe he goes chasing after
down his institute's white corridors like a rat in a maze!

Not to mention the History of the World in which
only the victors are mentioned in their Napoleonic dullness.

So the winner's witless pride will be preserved for us
and the loser's vague resentment, only here and there sweetened

by the illumined fuss of the sectarian preachers,
the comedians and dipsomaniacs. Stupidity,

you the often maligned, who in your slyness
often pretend to be stupider than you are, protector of all the frail,

only to the elect do you grant the rarest of your gifts,
the blessed simplicity of the simple.

They are the blank pages in your huge book
whose seal you'll not break for any of us.

Nice Sunday

The old whiskered gentleman,
frail of frame, look at him
sitting there on his little bench
in front of the shelter,
in front of his very own shelter.

Look at him sitting there, knitting,
muttering in the morning sun.
What did he say?
What did he say?
Nice Sunday today.
Nice Sunday today.

Now he will drop his knitting gear,
sniffing the air
he will cock his ear,
he will watch out
for someone coming up
to bash in his head.

Look, he picks up his needles again,
humming to himself:
Nobody there.
Nobody there.
Nice Sunday today.

[HME]

Flight of Ideas (I)

As though immediately beyond Helsinki
or Las Palmas all were quite different,
removals everywhere, ideas of flight.
Entire localities are mislaid.

In floodlight behind barriers,
the spastics of power
bent over maps. Then
a new stroke of history,
and it starts up again.

For decades a stored-up hatred.
Intentions hardly count.
More nomads than before
stagger across the streets.

What isn't needed, most things,
is left behind, bulky lumber,
sewing machines, collected works.

You, too, old man, allow yourself to be moved,
move yourself. Despite all your love.
What for? What are you looking for? Dollars,
cassava, fun, munitions?
Or only your peace?
'I look for an explanation.'

He can think himself lucky who only
like you on the motorway
goes into a skid. Gauze
is always at hand, and blue light.

Elsewhere they say: The last plane
from Juba, Lubango, Phnom Penh
has just landed. Baby bottles,
bedding, suitcases that have burst –
End of message.

Something shredded in the minefield,
next to it an unwounded shoe,
rafts in the Caribbean,
everything comes per satellite,
is stored, i.e. forgotten.

Dream vacation or panic,
in either case trucks, caravans,
traffic jam, no overall perspective,
stop and go, throbbing hearts,

here and there a helicopter,
and in front of you the brake lights
of your ancestors, a chain
of red dots in the smog.

This war, too,
isn't over yet.

Asphodels

Funny, that gnostic
on the fourth floor
is still awake.
He knocks and knocks
on the heating pipe.
The mob in front of the window
has gone, and now
on top of everything it's starting to snow.

In the whole city
no shoe-laces are to be had.
The machine-gun fire where the banks are
has subsided.
But in the fridge there are
a couple of asphodels,
just in case.

Trek

This ancient species of those who pass by,
always on their way to new activities –
in the beginning, long ago, they travelled through the air,
in their laps a second brain, for at that time
they were still counting on a future;
later, covered all over with weapons,
behind caravans of dark sherpas
with tropical trunks they set out for the jungles;
then they ordered their coachmen to load
clothes bags and mandolins on mail coaches,
or they embarked and sailed off
till their teeth dropped out;
only when their refuges were on fire
did they abandon their furniture and their pots;
on snow-covered ridge paths they were seen
crossing the passes as pilgrims; their last muskets
dropped from their numb hands;
they dragged their carts over logged roads,
their babies on their backs, their residual possessions
bundled, a needle saved
a candle a knife a loaf;
till after long detours,
even now in flight,
they reached the goal of their pilgrimage,
a rectangle of loose soil
in which they vanished.

MIXED FEELINGS

Taking Russian Leave

One takes a seat. One does not speak.
The heating pipes only blubber and
detonate. It's dark. At your empty hand
one fixedly stares. A guess, oblique,

tells that the stupid soul's on strike
when what is brewing is an end,
which cold stares on the skin portend.
Ears roar. Blood pressure hits a peak.

One waits and waits. All right, then, says
the silent suitcase. Well you know
that this long minute can't recur.

Get up, before the dawn's first rays,
and do what you are prompted to
before the room is bare.

His Father's Ghost

Some evenings he sits there
as he used to do, slightly bowed,
humming at his table
under the iron lamp.
The Chinese ink pen skims
the graph paper.
Quietly, sure of itself,
it traces its black course.
At times he listens to me,
his snow-white hair inclined,
absently smiles, goes on drawing
towards his wondrous plan
which I cannot understand,
which he'll never complete.
I hear him hum.

In Praise of Violence

Of course we are all
resolutely against it,
in principle.
But when the city
bluishly quakes, at night
the summer thunderstorm
flares through groaning trees,
windows bang,
the fire brigade howls,
the water violently
splashes on to the tiles –

Ah, how it heartens us,
ten quadrupled megawatts
for which we are not to blame
and which, defenceless
in our warm beds,
we let pass over us.

Comrade Bartleby

'I would prefer not to.'
So it begins, unspectacularly,
one morning. It's only the
necktie, after all, that constricts,
the account statement, what's disturbing is
that the one animal
which constantly washes
has to wash constantly;

it's the relentless stupidity, too,
out there,
the irrepressible din
that wears it down, the one animal
which lets itself be celebrated
not for having been born,
once a year, no, but
for rising day after day –
for what reason? – till pensioned.

It doesn't lie in late.
From the heavier blows to the neck
it recoils, mutinies
against hunger. Hunger
would prefer to, would. It
makes the bones light.

No, the illumination
comes after eating.
Fits of apathy
that recur at seventeen,
like the 'flu, at thirty-seven,
at eighty, always anew:
'I would prefer not to.'

Too weary to lift
the knife.
A few days long
with the head to the wall

or three weeks, then
with knees that give way,
the first walk to the wash-basin,
to the wardrobe, back
to the endless advertisement spots
for assault and murder.

Bird's Eye View

Immune to dizziness
like an old roofer,
agile, not noticed much
by those who have their feet
on the ground of facts,
to conjure

without holding on,
with a practised grasp,
when all goes well,
high up
to bring off
an inconspicuous miracle,

yes, that,
seen all in all,
is a mug's game,
but here and there allows
slanting glances downward,
into smaller abysses,
rooms

where, as the case may be,
women with vacuum cleaners
or moaning lovers
in their way,
but with touching zeal,
contend with
the force of gravity.

A Sort of Revelation

The galvanic tremor
deep in the sympathetic nerve
when something silken
rustles down.
Chemical turbulence of the soul.
Then this faint wheezing
in the dark – wheezing,
that is, 'a respiratory sound
of an almost piping nature'.

Fleeting, not to be grasped,
a sudden gift,
a sign of returned love
that none of us deserves.

It passes understanding
what's so sublime
about a woman's bare backside.

On the Algebra of Feelings

I often have the feeling (intense,
obscure, indefinable etc)
that the I is not a fact
but a feeling
I can't get rid of.

I tend it, give it a free run,
reciprocate it, from case to case.
But it's only one among many.

The mass of feelings is countably infinite,
i.e. they can be numbered in principle
ad infinitum or nauseam.

The number of jealousy
evidently is seven.
Fear, too, is a prime.
And I have the vague feeling
that humiliation
bears 188 on its forehead –
a number with no qualities.

And the feeling of being numbered
presumably has long been numbered,
only what for and by whom?

The sublime feeling of anger
occupies a different room
in Hilbert's Hotel
to the feeling
of being above anger.

And only those who can apply themselves
to the abstract feeling
for abstraction know
that in some very bright nights
it will assume the value $\sqrt{-1}$.

Then again it sends a shiver
down my spine, the feeling
of being a parcel,
that feelingless, furry feeling
which threatens to make one's tongue burst
after the injection,
when it probes the shape of a tooth,
or embarrassment
with its pervasive taste of lead,
the powerful feeling of powerlessness
which incessantly tends towards zero,
and the false feeling
of true sensibility
with its abominable continued fraction.

Then I am filled
with a cross-section of mixed feelings,
guilty, alien, euphoric, lost,
all at the same time.

To the highest of feelings alone
the I would not be equal.
Instead of looking for upsurges
with the threshold ∞,
it would rather
be overcome for one minute
by the shudder of icily hot water
under the shower, whose number
no one has yet deciphered.

Polaroid, Dissolving

More rarely you hear the hunting-horn sound.
And expressions like renunciation,
voluptuousness, bliss
hardly ever now reach your ears.
Slate pencil certificate of confession sealing-wax –
lost to you, lost.

The women of the past
slowly dissolve,
growing paler and paler
in the emulsion of the years.

That mourning turns white
and merges in whiteness,
that revenge's colour fades
and greed melts down –
if only that were all,
O beautiful soul!

But even weariness
you will grow weary of,
and of sorrow, pain.

Sit-down Strike

The Buddha takes to his legs.
The herald jogs along behind.
The fixed stars undulate.
Progress fidgets in the lay-by.
The snail loses its way, running.
The rocket limps.
Eternity limbers up for its final spurt.

I do not budge.

Leaving Aside

The limping janitor in the Institute
for Medieval Manuscript Studies
with his vacuum cleaner, born
in Bukovina before the wars
and with a previous conviction for child abuse;
the pregnant black woman
with her gigantic headphone, who
gabbles prayers wildly in Washington Square;
the lonely water tank on the roof,
how it rusts and rusts;
the double-breasted suits in silver buses
behind tinted glass;
and the gall-bladder sufferer with his suitcases
looking for a three-room flat
for his butterfly collection:
anyone who can't leave those aside
is no theorist.
All around them carefree murders occur.
The larger the perspective,
the smaller everything grows.

In front of the traffic lights wait the souls,
move, lightly as flies,
wait. The feeling of feelinglessness
at the car park, the motives
and the desires mislaid on the way,
the question, what has become of I
and, leaving that aside, the explanations
which, water-tight, pass by
as over the water tank on the flat roof
of the Institute does the Goodyear airship
high above Thirteenth Street.

Minimal Programme

Relinquishment, renunciation, asceticism –
that would be saying too much.

It's overwhelming, how much one can do without.
To take no notice of special offers
is pure delight. To turn up nowhere,
to refrain from most things –

a gain in knowledge by a waving aside.
Only one who overlooks many things

can see this thing and that.
The I – a hollow shape

defined by what it omits.
What one can hold fast,

what holds one fast
is the least of all things.

A Few Idle Lines

Never did we do less damage than at that period
when over long afternoons we slowly got drunk,
and were never so harmless, except when asleep,
as on those days we spent in confused discussion;
by the evening we'd forgotten everything we had said.
Yes, that was fabulous, how we sat around for days,
luxuriously lazy out of sheer unselfishness, looking on
while what we had received wastefully, gently vanished.

Rush-hour Traffic

In all congested areas
bodies wander about
with something to do.
Behind the thinker's brow
revolutionising plans.
They concern election lists,
extra-marital opportunities,
toupee shops.

No time, with the best will in the world,
like ancestors or ghosts
who need no upkeep
and no conversation
apart from intentions
to hover

or only to
roll themselves up
like that cat
on the carpet
unimportantly given up
to the unfathomably breathing
calm metabolic process.

Disappointed

By Mummy, who turned her back on her brawling brat
in favour of more alluring phenomena
and by the good Lord, who never showed due consideration
for our inclinations;
by the neighbours, who forgot to water our flowers;
after the promising first successes on all fronts
by the war; by Communism; by the fortune-teller;
by the High Court, which never did see
how much we were in the right;
by that mutual coming together
usually looked for in bed but not always found;
by the sweeper botching a penalty;
by the perishableness of the flesh,
by the extreme unction – and generally
disappointed we were, gravely disappointed, our whole lives long.

A marvel, therefore, that our whole lives long, always anew
we believed there was goodness in people – and generally.

Et Ego

Those tropical evenings in Thessaloniki
and the white nights by the Ofotfjord –
do you remember?

Certainly I remember.
But what did those amount to
compared with the weekend in Minnesota,
submerged in the new snow,
or with the full moon above Stockelsdorf-Krumbeck,
postal district of Pronstorf, in the Bad Segeberg region –
do you remember?

Certainly I remember.
But I don't remember
why.

Flight of Ideas (II)

Something you can hold on to –
why not? Passport number,
place of work, 'official revelation'.
True, getting a life sentence
is no solution either.
Optimism: a Münchhausen problem.

Do you move
or are you moved?
Detours, looping routes
on the phase chart of feelings.

What you were you can't remain,
not there, sticking to your gun,
sticking to the cause either
(what cause?).
No, you must let that be.

But what then? A roof, a word,
a hide-out, a way back,
or, when darkness falls,
at least a mat –
everyone looks for that.

Curiously porous,
your ideas of flight.
They love, fight, fold up,
intermingle, by innate compulsion.
You're a halfcast.

(Blue-black, pink, olive –
at one time, in Lima, the victors
distinguished more than twenty colours,
half, quarter or eighthcast,
zambigos, zambopretos,
zamboclaros and *saltratás.*)

Thrown together in beds,
on battlefields. 'Life' –
an oscillator always short of equilibrium.
Intentions hardly count.

We don't remain one of us.
Things won't remain what they were.
So much remains certain. Everything else
remains to be seen.

Persuasive Talk

At every possible opportunity
to be British or Left or masculine
or Catholic or young or yellow-skinned
or intelligent, or the contrary –
not very productive, my dear!
To spend your life walking about as a sandwich man
for your own qualities,
that can't be necessary.
A poorly pigmented epidermis,
after all, is not a profession,
and, as for that,
even love for your profession
can be exaggerated.

But I can't
get out of my skin, can I?

True enough. But that's no reason
for making a fuss about
your famous identity
that is no more
than a tinkling bell
and a clattering in the wind.
You could try something different.
It's the attempt – say not
the struggle nought availeth – that matters.

New Man

This new man
looks alien.

Agreeable,
this changed appearance.

'His father's spitting image.'
One hopes not.

He works hard,
emits noises.

We can't make out
what he wants.

Breathes, digests,
creeps, moans.

Halting he grows aware
of duality.

Clambers up words,
tries out

seesawing, swinging motions,
recklessness, fear.

Cleverer than us
one day, he staggers us.

Then, while
slowly we die,

unstoppably he grows
more and more like us.

DIVERSIONS UNDER THE CRANIUM

Self-demolishing Speech Act

I'm not saying anything, he says,
and, fidgeting in his chair,
he claims: I do not move.
I keep silent, he shouts. I'm asleep.
I promise never to make a slip
of the tongue. With consummate ease
I refute all my refutations. I am,
he proclaims, the most modest of men,
devoid of vanity. He protests
that he does not speak English.
Never, he says, would I refer to myself.
I am wrong maintaining that I am right
when I maintain that I'm wrong,
et cetera. That I would ever stutter
is out of the question. Altogether
credible and unaware of myself,
I think that I may rightfully claim
that I never contradict myself. I
am absent. I'm neither here nor th-th-th-there.

[HME]

Balancing Act

How on earth does he bring it off,
this limping angel,
to walk, to walk, to walk
for decades
on two lonely legs
without losing consciousness
or succumbing
to the horizontal...

A sort of tight-rope dance,
stumbling teetering plunging a hundred times over,
all painfully learnt;
a dizzying career,
a swinging and staggering,
left leg down up right leg back,
defying gravity.

Deep inside the skull
the gyrocompass,
a billowing field of antennae
in the maze.

The body does not know
what it does when walking.
If it knew
it would be lost.

Bifurcations

All things that put out twigs,
branches: delta lightning lung,
roots, synapses, fractions,
family or decision-making trees;
all things that multiply
and at the same time diminish –

not to be grasped,
too variously rich
for this sparrow brain,
this fortuitous link
in an infinite series
which, behind the back
of the one who instead of thinking
is thought, puts out
its twigs and branches.

Neuronic Nexus

Think of a baobab tree,
gigantic, with copious branchwork,
and people it in your mind
with thousands of tiny monkeys;
imagine how they clamber,
swing, how, clutching one another,
they sway from branch to branch,
till they let themselves drop,
sniff the air, couple, doze –
think of it, O poor thinker.

Then again they leap,
with a rushing litheness, electrically teem,
totter and crash down;
or they sit there, just like that,
slack, and dreamily scratch themselves
before the next assault. – Pity the one
out to describe all this!

Laugh, be startled, amazed,
but, before it drives you mad,
stop thinking about the act of thinking.

Under the Skin

There's a darker universe
under the skin,
unthinkingly
pumping away, seething,
kneading, labouring
while you're asleep:
plutonic unrest,
earth- and sea-quakes,
grand chemistry,
densely packed disasters.

Your interior jungle
is humid, off-colour,
vastly ramified,
age-old and hot.
A primal soup
fraught with a teeming mass
of bizarre parasites
proliferating, mutating
and withering away.

Aeons of geology
in fast forward motion,
and you don't even notice.

You are prostrate,
shallow of breath.
Your mind is absent,
drugged blind. The surgeon,
probe in hand,
is the only one to observe,
enormously magnified onscreen,
the organs' commotion.

[HME]

What the Doctors Say

The Heimlich manoeuvre,
a sudden pressure
on the pit of the stomach,
can be very helpful.

Manuel García,
singing teacher by profession,
was the first (1855)
to see his own vocal chords
vibrate, in a mirror.

All the gear in your mouth
permits deep insight:
epiglottis, tongue follicles,
the blind fossula,
opener and shutter.

The doctors know:
slack paralysis
and taut paralysis
are very different matters.

The doctors say:
heart and kidneys,
if they don't hurt,
are silent.

Norwegian Timber

Older than the unknown hand
lying on the table
it is, than the bones in the bed,
older than the eye the board
cut, planed, joined
by an unknown man,
painted by another
with unknown faces;

older than the wooden house over there,
at night, on the other side of the lake,
blurred, only a single window
lit up, in summer rain, from which
an unknown man looks at me,
naked, pale, blurred;

then the light goes out,
and only the timber, the timber
on which the rain drums,
the timber with its ducts,
rays and whorls,
heartwood and sapwood, smells,
groans, cracks, and stays.

More About a Tree

That silver birch over there, sun-flecked.
Don't move. Look
at the deviations: green from green,
matt from shiny, the leaf
darker on the surface than below
above. Nothing repeats itself.
Every nerve ripples as the breeze does
on the skin. The whole thing wavers,
straightens out, almost unchanged
but not quite.

It seesaws, dances, spins:
'pathological sets',
functions without derivation,
intermittent tracks in the phase space.

The leaves bend what bends them,
the wind, twist it
into flitting eddies
you cannot see. Let your
feeble brain calculate
till it quakes, whirrs, capsizes,
capitulates in face of the eddy
of appearances, and straightens again
like the silver birch before
your eyes, almost unchanged
but not quite.

Taxonomy

Grass, says the other,
what do you mean by grass?
Do you mean corn grass
or couch grass? I see,
you can't tell a sedge
from a sweet vernal grass,
the fescue from the slender brome grass?

Go and look!
Take a good look at the bulbous meadow-grass missed
and don't miss the cock's-foot grass –
there it grows, on marshy ground,
with its tiny violet flowers.
Then, my dear fellow, come back
and speak.

– Hatred, the one replied,
what do you mean by hatred?
What do you really mean
when you talk of love, or fear?
Take a good look at this bog-weed.
Then, my dear fellow, come back
and speak.

– I can't find the words,
said the other
and left.

On the Problem of Reincarnation

The fly bothers me.
I observe the fly,
I describe it,
the way its tactile parts work,
its three-jointed antennae,
the proboscis probing,
sucking, scooping
with fleshy lips.
The veins of the wing are ashen,
their brilliant scales
are glittering in the sun.
Tarsi, claws, bristles
aquiver with energy.
The twice four thousand lenses
of its enormous eyes
observe me.
How hairy it is!
It does not seem bothered
by my describing it.

It's the spitting image
of another fly, right here
on my desk, enshrined
in amber, which in its lifetime
never bothered any of us.
How did it manage to return
after hundreds of millions
of generations,
its black-checkered abdomen
quivering, absolutely unchanged.

It bothers me.
I chase it away –
that fly, not this one.

In its next incarnation
there will be no one around
to describe the likeness
between fly and fly.
It does not bother me
that nobody will be there
to chase it away.

[HME]

Flight of Ideas (III)

That things don't remain what they were
is true of stones, too.
The mountain range expands, flows,
pulsates, rushes, splits,
if only very slowly.
What does slowness mean
for a mountain?

Energies under the earth's crust,
under the cranium. Do you see
how all of it shifts,
mingles, folds, expands,
even that which you cannot see?

'The concept of totality
exists in theory,
not in life.'
Beneath us, in graves,
quite a few things accumulate.

Science, too, is porous,
breathes heavily, darts in panic
through its institute; he, too,
the biologist, teachable and confused
like his guinea-pig, searches
until, rarely enough, alas,
he releases the reward.

Then, a brief illumination,
an eruption of happiness,
flickering, on the way
to new eclipses.

Yes, do go and inspect the rubbish dumps
north of our city,
wallow in them, you augur,
fallen theologian
of offal!

An intoxicating fragrance.
Much of it, of course, poisonous,
like nature, like you and me;
mutated seeds, rank growth, viruses –
you can tell by the leaves
with spots, a mosaic
of dissolution,
pink, blue-black, olive,
deviations, incalculable
as orbits in the sky.

Multi-layered our joys smoulder.
All that's unconscious
gathers here, labelled.
Yes, and orders there are, too,
warnings. Oh, you do your best?
What does that amount to?
Intentions hardly count.

You move house, flee,
mix with that
which is the case.

You'd better be prepared
for complications.
We don't remain what we are.

A

Before you say B, linger a while,
listen, consider
what you said. A vowel
that signifies little,
sets much in motion.
Once you've opened your mouth
you propel your mortal frame
to endeavours
of cosmic complexity:
entire cascades of stimuli,
calculations, turbulences
behind the back of the one
who is I – not to mention
the brain
that does not speak
and laughs at all science.

Differently from anyone else
you have said A.
Not for the first time
but a millionfold
you have produced it,
this sound, loudly, haltingly,
at every possible pitch, in a whisper,
palatally, singing, straining,
at the doctor's, astonished,
overcome, mournful –
saying nothing, strictly speaking,
and not once,
strictly speaking, did you
repeat yourself.

Compared to you, technology
is a botching, rubble, lumber.
You can't even guess
how perfect you are –
unless it is when you're hoarse,
have the hiccups or cancer.
What you've lost is
the devoutness of beginnings.
No omega is in sight.

Humble-bee, Bumble-bee

Amazing, how she takes off
quivering with energy,
how she rises
and, softly thudding,
hurls herself towards light
against the window-pane.

After the crash,
another attempt,
more practised in the approach,
more caution, less vehemence.
To freedom, to the sun.
The glass remains impenetrable.

The antennae more and more limp,
hopeless sallies.
The fall mere routine.
A life for art's sake.

Till she just lies there,
faintly twitching,
on the window-sill,
that furry singer.

The Renaissance Specialist

An astrologer of extinguished stars.
Under his green lampshade
at Princeton, New Jersey.
he reconstructs vanished codices,
observant as a police spy,
wide-awake as a forger.

Like an excited lover
he feels his way in, from the inside,
with touches close to the skin,
into the warm glove
of tradition,
into the rind of dead brains.

His Latin effortlessly keeps pace
with the night-long banquets
in Florence or Bologna
among painters, mathematicians,
cardinals, immersed
in saturnine conversation.

Then he puts out the light,
opens the magnetic barrier
and down the freeway drives home
in the glowing sodium haze
of whip-shaped lamps.

Congratulation to a Lady Called Elizabeth

For your birthday once more
the album leaf in A-minor,
'familiar to every beginner' –
one waves it aside –
one more Master-degree thesis
on the history of the reception
of Elizabethan literature –
not for us!
Reminiscences à la Romy Schneider –
candy-floss of the 19th century –
a candle for the Landgravine of Thüringen –
but roses don't satisfy hunger –,
or how about an air ticket
to Lubumbashi (Zaïre),
renamed long ago, the heat murderous
and the villas burnt down:
altogether, no more festschrifts, please,
one stays at home, where
perhaps one is needed still.

Old Medium

What you see in front of you,
ladies and gentlemen,
this swarm
is letters.
Please bear with me.
Please bear with me.
Hard to decipher,
I know, I know.
Too much to ask.
You'd rather have it audio-visual,
digital and in colour.

But anyone really serious about
virtual reality,
for instance:
Shall I compare thee...
or: April is the cruellest
month, or else:
He that is down needs fear no fall,
can make do with very little.

Twenty-six
of these black-on-white dancers,
quite without graphic display
and CD-ROM,
for hardware the stub of a pencil –
that's all.

My apologies.
Accept them, please.
The last thing I wanted was to make excessive demands.
But you know how it is:
some of us never learn – or unlearn.

Paolo di Dono, known as Uccello

Paolo di Dono, a barber's son,
got lost in a new science,
a new sort of magic: perspective.
'He worries nature,' they said,
'until the mind is filled
with difficulties and grows awkward.'

Battles, tournaments. The fighters
impenetrable at the moment
before death. Precision
in uncertainty. Hares, greyhounds,
grasshoppers: phantasms
beneath the sickle moon,
in the orange grove whirlwinds,
hooves and feet.

Unicorns on the pennons,
winged helmets, tall hoods
of wickerwork, upholstered
with hair, the lining scarlet,
and iron horsemen
chased by shawms
on gigantic wooden horses,
green, white and pink,
with panic-stricken eyes.

Each one thinks
himself the centre.
All but the painter.
He works 'calmly, cleanly
like the silkworm
on its thread', poor,
useless, retiring,
wild, 'he casts
time behind time
and worries nature'.

A Backward Glance at Painting

Peniculus, little penis, in the vernacular:
Willy, familiar since the Stone Age.
Reed, silk, human hair, ostrich feathers
all in the service of art
turned into brushes and quills.

The white boar, the hare, the bear,
squirrel, too, sable and badger,
beaver, otter, ermine –
always they had to shed hair
for the gold leaf, the stippling,
the cropped, dispensing, pointed, oil
and bristle brush. Yes, undoubtedly

all this was needed, all that existed
at that time, when there were painters who painted.

For Karajan and Others

Three men in stiff hats
in front of Kiev Main Station –
trombone, accordion, saxophone –

in the vapours of an October night
that hesitates between two trains,
between disaster and disaster:

they play for tired people, who very devoutly
bite into their warm piroshki
and wait, wait,

heart-rending tunes, worn
like the jackets and greasy
as their hats, and if you

had stood there, chilled, among alcoholics,
veterans, pickpockets,
you would have agreed with me:

Salzburg, Bayreuth and La Scala
don't compare all that favourably
with the Main Station of Kiev.

IN SUSPENSE

Presumption of Innocence

This seven-year-old girl on her trampoline,
how effortlessly, with her hair flying,
she gets the better of gravity;

the chef who, intent, the wooden spoon in his mouth,
licks, listens, waits for the flavour
behind the flavour to flow through his nostrils;

the hopelessly neglected tone-setter,
how with monkey-like relish
he hammers his cadenza into the keys;

the absent-minded couple in the midst of
syringes and beer cans on their clammy park bench
encased in each other;

the murderer who, beside himself with delight
at the ideal penalty-kick, forgets
his mission, his alibi, the place of the crime;

or the fat old woman over there who, blinking,
scratches herself, and ecstatically
plays with her sandy toes;

and the bent shoe-shine man, how he basks
in the reflection of the radiance which his saliva
has bewitched the leather toe-cap to yield:

these beings happy to the point of unconsciousness —
for a moment it isn't their fault
that they're no ordinary animals.

Arterial Road

It is as though you'd unexpectedly woken up,
as though long enough you'd been out hunting
for that which escaped you,
as though you had really noticed
what is really there,
as though you had suddenly discovered something,
as though you'd discovered the philosopher's stone,
as though you'd discovered
what the philosopher's stone is good for,
as though it shone,
as though all were initiates whom you ran into
at this street corner like any other,
as though you were one of them –

till the second hand moves on one second,
the traffic light leaps from red to yellow,
and you drive on down the sign-posted road.

Inconspicuous Miracle

Of Lake Gennessaret
presumably he has never heard,
that seventy-year-old man at the traffic light.
His mother didn't go to church.
How slender are his chances
of getting safely across the pedestrian crossing
with that pom on its lead! A marvel
that he emerged at all
from neolithic times, that he
survived precipitate labour
back in those years at Leschnitz in Chelm,
Lésnica, Poland, today, in a barn
surrounded by snipers, then
the splintering ice on the pond,
aged seven, while skating,
later, years on the dole,
heavy barrage near Kursk, a stroke
in Mallorca, and yet a thousand times
that deadly roadway crossed
to buy milk – improbable,
let's say: ten squared minus nineteen,
for him to have got through
as far as today,
stumbling, but with dry feet
on his long, long foot journey
across Lake Gennessaret, of which he knows
no more than his little dog.

An Encounter of the Other Kind

The reasons for the massacre must be looked for in the 13th century.
That's what I read this morning at breakfast.

That bees are not deaf but hear with their antennae,
was made known in Stanford, California.

Neckties are now worn again a little wider;
this was proved to me by a junk mail missive from 33102 Paderborn.

Time is not a parameter but an operator,
my friend the philosopher confided to me.

Information learnt on a single Tuesday.
I recited it to the neighbour's cat.

Her flame-coloured striations gleamed in the sun.
She kept her eyes fixed on me.

I sensed that her fur was electrically charged.
It was evident that she recognised me.

And yet she lived in a universe other than mine –
So it seemed to me. She mewed,

but what she knew about matter,
about space and time, she did not reveal.

One metaphysic grazed the other
when I shared my kipper with her.

Our decisions, hers and mine,
so it seemed to me, were reciprocally

unfathomable as those of the gods.

The Somnambulist Ear

How will you ever get to sleep again
when in the hour empty of human sounds
before the first light
the house knocks and scratches,
when you hear it murmur
behind the wall?

These shots, do they come from a film
that nobody sees,
or is there someone dying on the staircase?
Something coos where no pigeon lives,
something sighs – an old refrigerator
or a pair of lovers long ago vanished?

In the vents the gas hisses.
Heavy furniture is shifted.
Something trickles. The steam ticks.
Water hurtles through the pipes.
Who's drinking, who's taking a shower?
Who's evacuating himself?

And when at last it's quiet –
the house holds its breath in terror –
you hear a whirring
almost beyond the audible,
phantasmally thin as the glittering ring
of an unstoppable meter

that revolves in the dark.

Was There Something

There was something good
just now,
somewhere else.
A pity
that it's so difficult
to remember
something good.
To know
how it really was.
How real it was.

It was, I think,
something quite ordinary,
something quite wonderful.
I saw it,
I think,
or smelled it
or touched it.

But whether it was
large or small,
new or old,
bright or dark,
I no longer know.

Only that it was better,
better by far
than what is there,
that much I still know.

Clinical Meditation

On the escalator, on the beach, in the shaving mirror:
everywhere the disabled, patients, people in need of care,
but no one is sick or demented. Obsolete
are the consumptives. No more talk
of chronic coryza, caked hearts and vapours.
What's become of the yellow gangrene?
Of the English malady and the scurvy?
Even afflictions don't last for ever.
Lost words that struck terror: dog's death,
hairworm and hymenoid brownness.
Restlessly the reactor of evolution looks
for new solutions, new hostages.
Even ailments improve
from year to year. The pharyngeal plague and blue erysipelas
can't keep pace
with progressive pathogens.
No red list mourns for tympanitis,
for the witches' braid or the scab.
Triumphantly science bends
over the whitest of beds
and mumbles its prayers for the dead.

Grace

Another of those foreign words, rarely to be heard
on the telephone. The exhausted vicar
with those syringes and condoms in his front garden
would be embarrassed to mention it.
In the contest of grace, we learn from the experts,
'little errors in the equipoise
can have a disastrous effect, as in
the coordination of the subordinate with that which should be
            superordinated,
the superordination of the coordinate with that which should be
            subordinated.
the subordination of the superordinate to that which should be
            coordinated'.

I can hardly believe that. There are other languages
in which for that grace and mere gracefulness
one and the same word serves. Created
and uncreated, actual and habitual,
edifying and medicinal grace:
who can distinguish between them?
On the other hand, a little gracefulness
would be something. The consummate feeling.
A little gracefulness would be better than nothing.
A little gracefulness would be enough for me.

The Visit

When I looked up from my blank page
there was an angel in the room.

A rather commonplace angel,
presumably of lower rank.

You cannot imagine, he said,
the degree to which you're dispensable.

Of the fifteen thousand hues of blue,
he said, each one makes more of a difference

than anything you may do
or refrain from doing,

not to mention the felspar
or the Great Magellanic Cloud.

Even the common plantain, unassuming
as it is, would leave a gap. Not you.

I could tell from his bright eyes –
he hoped for an argument, for a long fight.

I did not move. I waited in silence
until he had gone away.

[HME]

OSIRIS

(Outer Space Intelligence Research and Investigation System)

Tell me, why can't you
let night be night?

Because I am hungry.
Because I have to work.

Kindling splinters, torches, Bengal lights –
all these only to drudge?

To fiddle about, play-act, to dance.
Because otherwise the evenings would grow too long for me.

That's why you make half the planet
shine with your light-bulbs?

Because I don't want to go to bed. Out of fear.
Because I can't go to sleep.

Excuses! Other dark stars
are discreetly silent. All you want

is to be seen. The universe
is to take notice of you.

But that you were on this earth,
electrical fool, believe me,

no one but I ever noticed.

A Reproach

Irresponsible wastrel,
what did you do with those leaves?

With the feather-nerved, many-coloured leaves,
none like the other, therefore leaf
by leaf irreplaceable,
eroded by rot on the path and trodden
down in rain?

What were you thinking of?
Everywhere this precious refuse:
ingenious round snails,
brains,
elliptic galaxies –
not to mention
my uniquely valuable
spermatazoa:
all of them only a pastime,
scrap?

Maybe he will hear me,
that wastrel.
Many things are heard,
perhaps,
as a distant rustling,
a rustling in the leaves.

Addressee Unknown – *Retour à l'expéditeur*

Many thanks for the clouds.
Many thanks for the *Well-tempered Clavier*
and, why not, for the warm winter boots.
Many thanks for my strange brain
and for all manner of other hidden organs,
for the air, and, of course, for the claret.
Heartfelt thanks for my lighter and my desire
not running out of fuel,
as well as my regret, my deep regret.
Many thanks for the four seasons,
for the number e, for my dose of caffeine,
and, of course, for the strawberry dish
painted by Chardin, as well as for sleep,
for sleep quite especially, and,
last not least, for the beginning and the end
and the few minutes in between
fervent thanks,
even, if you like, for the voles out there in the garden.

[HME]

Nimbus

Another of those words
that have slipped away, quietly.
'Cloudlike splendour, imagined as investing
deities when they appeared on earth.'

Only among meteorologists,
from time to time, it is uttered
when low-hanging rain clouds
drift over the chemical steppe.

On such days I like to go
to the museum or, in high summer,
into a church, where it's cool,
and, unbelievingly, contemplate

the haloes of saints.

Flight of Ideas (IV)

That little pilgrim there
on her chaotic course,
this rambling, groping,
glimmering nothing –
what did they say the name was? –
and what could it be looking for,
the provisionally
immortal soul?

She grubs in refuse,
indefatigably, for bits of wisdom
that suddenly were gone,
crumbled away in endless permutations,
in mouldy paperbacks.

She can't stay put,
won't see the point,
simply can't grasp it,
that tiny pilgrim.

How she folds up, expands,
folds up like puff pastry
rolled by energies
from the heliosphere
and from the deeper layers
of her brain! No,

She can't desist,
mingles, by instinct,
by old habit,
with clouds, oceans, stars.

Never is she content with
that which is the case.
Yes, she says, I want to go back,
I want to go on, to no known goal
I move, I am moved,
for the time being, provisionally
I remain in suspense.

Of Life After Death

Later, when the turbines have stopped,
the neon signs are out,
when the first crack in the concrete appears
and slowly, slowly branches out –
a hair-thin pattern, illegible –;
when winged creatures come whirring in,
bringing diminutive capsules,
seeds, spores, from far away,
when saxifrage bursts through the works,
ants climb over the split cables
and the abandoned control points
are overshadowed by gigantic trees,
life runs riot again:
an extraordinarily sublime spectacle,
but far and wide there is no Piranesi
to people this Angkor Wat
with shepherds and courtiers on horseback.

The Entombment

Our mortal frame,
they call it.
But what did it hold?
The psychologist will say:
Your psyche.
Your soul,
the priest.
Your personality,
the personnel manager.

Furthermore,
there's the anima,
the imago, the daemon,
the identity and the Ego,
not to mention the Id
and the Super-Ego.

The butterfly which is to rise
from this very mixed lot
belongs to a species
about which nothing is known.

Selected Poems

by HANS MAGNUS ENZENSBERGER

translated by
HANS MAGNUS ENZENSBERGER & MICHAEL HAMBURGER

POETRY BOOK SOCIETY RECOMMENDED TRANSLATION

This German-English bilingual edition draws on several collections published by Enzensberger during the past thirty years, from *Language of the Country* (1960) to *Music of the Future* (1991), but excluding *Kiosk* (published by Bloodaxe in a separate English edition). It includes a large selection from *The Sinking of the Titanic*, which *The Guardian* called 'a brilliant fantasia on the foundering of western society'. For George Szirtes, writing in the *New Statesman*, it was 'a dramatic and philosophical statement of compulsive power...our emotions and our reason are driven along together as in the best of Brecht. We hear in Enzensberger the human voice amongst human voices, feel the extraordinariness of ordinary men.'

'Like Primo Levi, Enzensberger possesses in abundance the only possible antidote to encroaching madness and barbarity: an unshakeable faith in clear thinking, human decency, and the curious charm of the material world' – PETER FORBES, *Independent on Sunday*.

'He analyses with cool rage our world in which information about atrocities and commercial advertising issue indifferently from the same radio... Enzensberger's poetry is surprising and inevitable and haunts the mind. He re-creates experience in absolute terms, keeps our attention firmly focussed on what is, has been and will be important...he ranks with the few contemporary poets who understand the past as well as the present and have much to contribute to those who may still be literate in the future' – HARRY GUEST, *The North*.